Go The Extra Mile

With Strong Middle Fingers

Best of the Worst

Embarrassing Emails

Creative Insults

Dumbest Customers

www.ingramcontent.com/pod-product-compliance
Lightning Source LLC
Chambersburg PA
CBHW071212220526
45468CB00002B/575
9781791514860